DOCUMENTING U.S. HISTORY

THE
UNITED STATES CONSTITUTION

Liz Sonneborn

Heinemann
LIBRARY

Chicago, Illinois

www.capstonepub.com
Visit our website to find out more information about Heinemann-Raintree books.

To order:
☎ Phone 800-747-4992
📠 Visit www.capstonepub.com
to browse our catalog and order online.

© 2013 Heinemann Library
an imprint of Capstone Global Library, LLC
Chicago, Illinois

Edited by Abby Colich, Megan Cotugno, and Laura Hensley
Designed by Cynthia Della-Rovere
Original illustrations © Capstone Global Library Limited 2011
Illustrated by Oxford Designers & Illustrators
Picture research by Tracy Cummins
Originated by Capstone Global Library Limited
Printed and bound in China by CTPS

16 15 14 13 12
10 9 8 7 6 5 4 3 2 1

Library of Congress Cataloging-in-Publication Data
Sonneborn, Liz.
  The United States Constitution / Liz Sonneborn.
    p. cm.—(Documenting U.S. history)
  Includes bibliographical references and index.
  ISBN 978-1-4329-6752-9 (hb)—ISBN 978-1-4329-6761-1 (pb) 1. Constitutional history—United States—Juvenile literature. 2. United States. Constitution—Juvenile literature. I. Title.
    KF4541.S66 2013
    342.7302—dc23   2011037781

Acknowledgments
The author and publishers are grateful to the following for permission to reproduce copyright material: Alamy: p. 5 (© Michael Ventura); Corbis: pp. 37 (© Gregg Newton), 41 (© JIM LO SCALZO/epa); Getty Images: pp. 7 (Tom Williams/Roll Call), 9 (William Barnes Wollen), 14 (Universal History Archive), 15 (Stock Montage), 17 (MPI), 19 (Stock Montage), 21 bottom (Kean Collection), 22 (Hulton Archive); Library of Congress Prints and Photographs Division: pp. 10, 12, 13, 26, 35 bottom; National Archives: pp. 11, 23, 31, 32, 38; Official White House Photo: p. 42 (Pete Souza); Shutterstock: pp. 21 top (© Olivier Le Queinec), 28 (© fstockfoto), 33 (© Ryan Rodrick Beiler), 39 (© Jerric Ramos); The Granger Collection, NYC: pp. 24, 25, 27, 35 top.

Cover image of signing the United States Constitution in 1787 reproduced with permission from CORBIS (© Bettmann). Cover image of the Constitution reproduced with permission from National Archives.

Contents

Some words are printed in bold, **like this**. You can find out what they mean by looking in the glossary.

Sources of History

The U.S. Constitution is possibly the most important document in U.S. history. It established how the government of the United States works. It also set out certain basic rights that all U.S. citizens share.

Primary sources

The U.S. Constitution is an example of a **primary source**. Primary sources are written or made by someone living through a historical event. Like the Constitution, some primary sources are official documents. But more informal writings, such as diaries or letters, are also helpful to historians. By studying primary sources, historians can create a picture of how people lived in the past.

> "We the People of the United States, in Order to form a more perfect Union, establish Justice, insure domestic Tranquility [peace], provide for the common defence, promote the general Welfare, and secure the Blessings of Liberty to ourselves and our Posterity [future], do ordain and establish this Constitution for the United States of America."
>
> —*from the **preamble** (introduction) to the U.S. Constitution*

Documents, letters, diaries, and newspapers are just a few primary sources on display.

Not all primary sources are written down. Other types of primary sources include films, audio recordings, photographs, artwork, and even everyday objects like tools and toys. In fact, just about everything produced in an earlier time period can provide a clever historian with clues about times long ago.

You might not realize it, but every day you produce primary sources. Your text messages, your Facebook posts, and even your homework reveal things about you. If you saved all of these, a future historian might study them to learn about your times.

Archives

Important primary sources that survive usually end up in an **archive**. An archive is a place where primary sources are collected and carefully stored. For example, the original official copy of the U.S. Constitution is housed in the National Archives in Washington, D.C.

At archives, experts called **archivists** research the items in their collections. By studying and preserving primary sources, archivists ensure that future generations can see and learn from them.

Secondary sources

By studying primary sources, historians develop an understanding of the past. They often write down their ideas about other time periods in history books and textbooks. These are examples of **secondary sources**.

If you want to learn about another time, it makes sense to look at both primary and secondary sources. Each type serves a different purpose. In primary sources, people of another time period tell you about their lives in their own words or through the objects they made. In this way, you can feel a connection to people of the past. You might even be able to imagine how you would feel in their place.

Know It!

Recent technologies have created new types of primary sources. In the future, e-mails, computer files, and digital photographs will be among the things historians look at to learn about how we lived.

Secondary sources, on the other hand, help you see the big picture. By telling you the complete history of the time period, they can help you make sense of primary documents.

Museums and archives display many kinds of primary sources, including everyday objects from the past.

Governing the States

The U.S. Constitution set out rules for governing the United States. It was written in 1787, when the country was just 11 years old.

Under British rule

The United States was founded in 1776. Before then, there were 13 **colonies**. These colonies were ruled by the king of Great Britain and his representatives in North America.

By the late 1700s, many American **colonists** were tired of British rule. They were angry that the British government forced them to pay high taxes. At the same time, the British did not allow the colonists to have much of a say in their own government. Many colonists thought they could do a better job of governing themselves.

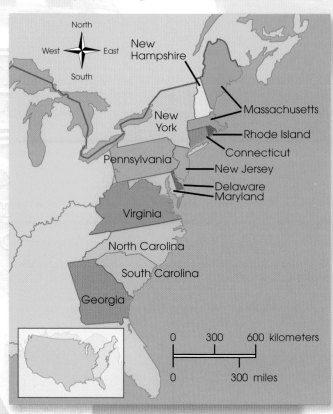

The 13 colonies were located along what is now the eastern coast of the United States.

May 14, 1607
Jamestown, the first permanent British settlement in what is now the United States, is founded.

Know It!

Some of the men who helped write the U.S. Constitution fought in the **Revolutionary War**. They included George Washington and Alexander Hamilton.

American colonists fought the British army during the Revolutionary War.

The Revolutionary War

Some Americans began to protest against British rule. At one protest in 1773, called the Boston Tea Party, they threw tea into the harbor of Boston, Massachusetts. The American colonists were upset that the British government had placed a tax on tea.

Tensions between the colonists and British grew. Finally, in April 1775, colonists and British troops exchanged fire in the towns of Lexington and Concord in Massachusetts Colony. These battles marked the beginning of the Revolutionary War (1775–1783). By fighting this war, the colonists hoped to win their independence.

December 16, 1773
American colonists protest British taxes at the Boston Tea Party.

April 19, 1775
The Revolutionary War begins with the battles of Lexington and Concord.

The Second Continental Congress

A month after the war began, leaders of the American colonies met in Philadelphia, Pennsylvania. The meeting was called the Second Continental **Congress**. The **delegates**, or representatives, from all the colonies discussed what they should do next.

One of the delegates from Virginia was Richard Henry Lee. He said that the delegates should make a formal declaration (announcement) that they were now free from British rule. Thomas Jefferson, another Virginia delegate (see the box), was chosen to write it.

Thomas Jefferson
(1743–1826)

Born in Virginia, Thomas Jefferson was a man of many talents. He was an accomplished politician, planter, lawyer, architect, and musician. It was because of his writing skills, however, that he was chosen to **draft** the Declaration of Independence. Jefferson later served as the first secretary of state and the third president of the United States.

May 10, 1775
The Second Continental Congress first meets.

On July 4, Congress approved Jefferson's document. It was called the Declaration of Independence. The declaration said that the colonies were now states in a new nation—the United States of America.

Forming a central government

Lee made another proposal during the Second Continental Congress. He wanted Congress to create a central government. Each state had its own government and its own laws. But a central government would be able to make laws for all the states. It would help the states deal with issues that affected the entire country.

In the Declaration of Independence, Thomas Jefferson famously wrote that "all men are created equal."

July 4, 1776
Members of the Second Continental Congress approve the Declaration of Independence.

The Articles of Confederation

The Second Continental Congress formed a committee to come up with a plan for the central government. It drafted a document called the **Articles** of **Confederation**. After much discussion, Congress approved the Articles in late 1777.

Congress then sent copies of the document to each state's **legislature**, or lawmaking body. The legislatures had to review and **ratify** (approve) the Articles before the new central government could be established. The process went on for years. Finally, the Articles of Confederation went into effect on March 1, 1781.

The British army surrendered at Yorktown, Virginia, in 1781. Two years later, a peace treaty (agreement) formally ended the Revolutionary War.

November 15, 1777
The Second Continental Congress approves the Articles of Confederation.

March 1, 1781
The Articles of Confederation go into effect.

October 19, 1781
The British army surrenders at Yorktown, Virginia.

A weak government

The government set up under the Articles of Confederation was not very powerful. For instance, it was unable to collect taxes, which the country needed to pay its war debts. It also had little authority in settling disputes between states.

The Revolutionary War ended in 1783, with a victory for the American colonists. After fighting a war for freedom, they did not want to set up a government as powerful as the British king had been. So the states wanted the central government to be fairly weak. That way, it would not be able to interfere with state governments.

ARTICLES

OF

Confederation

AND

Perpetual Union

BETWEEN THE

S T A T E S

OF

NEW HAMPSHIRE, MASSACHUSETTS BAY, RHODE ISLAND, AND PROVIDENCE PLANTATIONS, CONNECTICUT, NEW YORK, NEW JERSEY, PENNSYLVANIA, DELAWARE, MARYLAND, VIRGINIA, NORTH CAROLINA, SOUTH CAROLINA, AND GEORGIA.

WILLIAMSBURG:
Printed by ALEXANDER PURDIE.

Know It!

Roger Sherman of Connecticut helped draft both the Articles of Confederation and the U.S. Constitution. He was the only **Founding Father** to sign both of these documents and the Declaration of Independence.

September 3, 1783
The signing of the Treaty of Paris marks the end of the Revolutionary War.

The Constitutional Convention

Almost from the beginning, it was clear that there were serious problems with the **Articles** of **Confederation**. The government it established proved to be far too weak. It did not even have the authority to force the states to obey laws they did not like.

Revising the Articles

Some leaders wanted to **revise**, or change, the Articles. One of them was James Madison (see the box) of Virginia. He organized the Annapolis **Convention** in 1786. There, representatives from five states agreed that the United States needed a stronger central government.

James Madison (1751–1836)

James Madison is often called the Father of the Constitution. As a congressman from Virginia, he helped persuade his colleagues to abandon the Articles of Confederation and establish a stronger central government. He **drafted** much of the U.S. Constitution himself. In 1808 he was elected the fourth president of the United States.

September 11, 1786
State representatives meet for the Annapolis Convention.

The Constitutional Convention was held in the Pennsylvania State House, also known as Independence Hall.

Congress responded by organizing the Philadelphia Convention. (This meeting later became known as the Constitutional Convention.) In May 1787, 55 **delegates** from all the states except for Rhode Island gathered at the Pennsylvania State House.

As the meeting began, the delegates set out to make changes to the Articles of Confederation. But soon they agreed that there was no easy way to fix the document. They instead decided to get rid of the Articles altogether. The delegates would write an entirely new constitution that would set out rules for a better, stronger U.S. government.

May 14, 1787
Delegates from all the states, except for Rhode Island, gather in Philadelphia to discuss revising the Articles of Confederation.

The Virginia Plan

Even before the Constitutional Convention began, the delegates from Virginia wrote a draft of the Constitution. It became known as the Virginia Plan. The Virginia delegates proposed a dramatic change in the U.S. government.

Under the Articles of Confederation, the only government body was Congress. But under the proposed Virginia Plan, the new government would have three branches—the executive, legislative, and judicial. The **executive branch** would operate the government. The **legislative branch** would make laws. The **judicial branch** would hear court cases of national importance.

The Virginia Plan distributed power among all three branches of government. That way, no one branch could become too powerful. This system was meant to reassure U.S. leaders who did not want a strong central government.

Know It!

The delegates of the Constitutional Convention chose George Washington from Virginia to act as the meeting's president. Washington had been the general in charge of the colonial army during the **Revolutionary War**.

May 25, 1787
The Philadelphia Convention (now known as the Constitutional Convention) begins.

16

The 55 delegates to the Constitutional Convention met six days a week throughout much of the summer of 1787.

Discussions and disagreements

But many delegates were still uneasy with the Virginia Plan. They were especially upset that a president would be in charge of an executive branch. A president sounded a little too much like a king to them. Some delegates proposed that instead of one president, the country should have three—one to head each branch of the U.S. government.

May 29, 1787
Delegates from Virginia present the
Virginia Plan to the Convention.

Making laws

The delegates also disagreed about how the national **legislature** should be set up. According to the Virginia Plan, the new Congress would be divided into two sections, or houses. These eventually became known as the House of Representatives and the Senate.

The debate centered on how the members of these bodies should be chosen. Some delegates wanted the state legislatures to select them. But others wanted the members to be directly elected by voters.

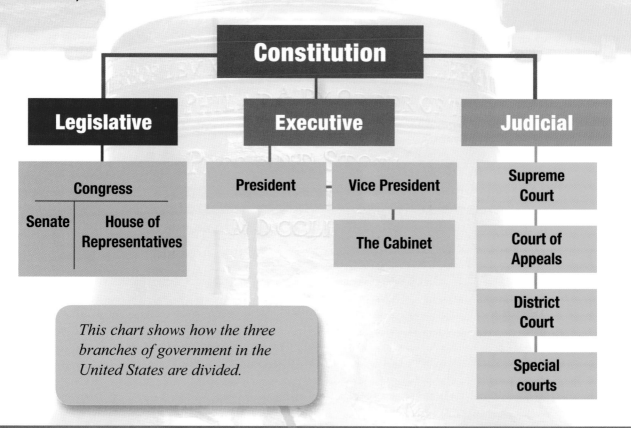

Constitution

Legislative

Congress

Senate | House of Representatives

Executive

President — Vice President

The Cabinet

Judicial

Supreme Court

Court of Appeals

District Court

Special courts

This chart shows how the three branches of government in the United States are divided.

Choosing members of Congress

The delegates also fought over how many members of Congress would represent each state. Many thought the number should be based on the state's population. Under this system, a state with a large population would have more Congressional representatives than a state with a small one. Not surprisingly, states with small populations did not like this plan. Their delegates thought that every state, no matter its size, should have the same number of representatives.

Finally, Roger Sherman of Connecticut (see the box) came up with a plan the delegates could agree on. He proposed that, in one house (now the House of Representatives), a state's population would determine its number of representatives. In the other (now the Senate), all states would have the same number.

Roger Sherman (1721–1793)

Roger Sherman worked as a lawyer and a storekeeper before entering politics. He served in the Connecticut legislature and later the Continental Congress during the Revolutionary War. As a delegate to the Constitutional Convention, he suggested the rules for how members of Congress would be elected. He later served in both the House of Representatives and the Senate.

July 16, 1787
The Constitutional Convention votes to accept Roger Sherman's plan for selecting members of Congress.

Writing the Document

After three weeks, the **delegates** of the Constitutional **Convention** wrote their first **draft** of the Constitution. But their hard work was far from over. They still had many smaller issues to work out about how the government should operate.

The delegates debated these issues until late July. They then selected five members to serve on the Committee of Detail. This committee was charged with **revising** the first draft based on their discussions.

Know It!

Even though it was hot outside, the delegates kept all the doors and windows shut in their meeting room. They did not want anyone to overhear their discussions. Each delegate also had to swear not to talk about the meetings with outsiders.

Revising and rewording

The Committee of Detail delivered its second draft to a Philadelphia printer. He printed 60 copies. Sixteen of these are now preserved in various museums and **archives**, including the Library of **Congress** and the National Archives.

June 13, 1787
Convention delegates create the first draft of the Constitution.

June 23, 1787
Convention delegates establish the Committee of Detail to revise the Constitution.

The Constitutional Convention was held in the Assembly Room in Independence Hall. This was the same room where the Declaration of Independence was signed.

The printer promised not to tell anyone anything about the document. The delegates did not want any information about their meetings to leak out to the public before the Constitution was in its final form.

With this second draft in hand, the delegates went back to work. They looked closely at the document, thinking about every word. They wanted to make sure that the document said exactly what they wanted it to say.

This draft, handwritten by Pennsylvania delegate James Wilson, is the earliest version of the Constitution we have today.

August 6, 1787
A Philadelphia printer prints a second draft of the Constitution.

21

The Committee of Style

Based on these discussions, another committee—the Committee of Style—took on the task of writing a third draft. The earlier one had 23 **articles**, or sections. The committee thought that arrangement was too complicated. They grouped sections together so that their new draft had only seven articles.

The engrossed copy

The delegates had 500 copies of this draft printed. They also had an **engrossed** copy made. An engrossed document is its final, official version.

Gouverneur Morris
(1752–1816)

Representing Pennsylvania at the Constitutional Convention, a man named Gouverneur Morris had the biggest hand in choosing the exact wording used in the Constitution. A lawyer by trade, he was one of the youngest members of the Continental Congress. After briefly serving in the Senate, he retired from politics.

September 8, 1787
The Committee of Style is formed to craft a final version of the U.S. Constitution.

September 15–17, 1787
Jacob Shallus produces the engrossed copy of the U.S. Constitution.

The convention hired Jacob Shallus to write the engrossed copy. Shallus was the clerk for Pennsylvania's **legislature**. Shallus wrote the U.S. Constitution out by hand. His pen was made from a feather with its tip carved to a point. Dipping the tip in ink, he used a fancy writing style called calligraphy. Shallus did not write on paper, because it could wrinkle or tear too easily. Instead, he wrote the Constitution on **parchment**. Parchment was made from a stretched animal skin scraped of all its fur.

Shallus had only two days to do the job. Hurrying his work, he made a few mistakes. He had to add a paragraph at the end of the document listing them. It is called the errata paragraph. *Errata* means "errors" in the ancient Latin language.

This is the engrossed copy of the Constitution. The phrase "We the People" appears in large letters on the Constitution to show the importance of voters in the new government.

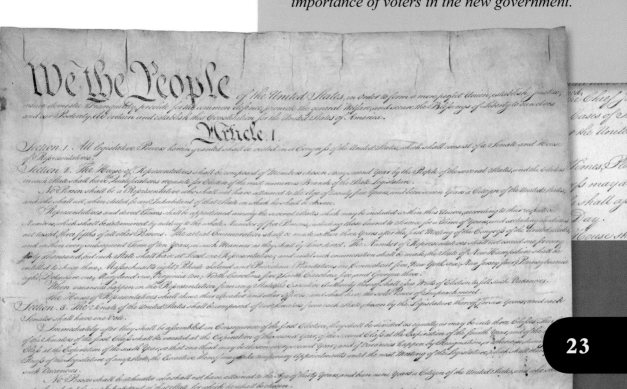

To the states

The third draft of the U.S. Constitution was also the last. On September 17, 1787, 39 of the members of the Constitutional Convention who were present signed the document. Three delegates refused to sign their names. They were still convinced that the Constitution gave the central government too much power.

George Mason of Virginia was one of three delegates to the Constitutional Convention who refused to sign the U.S. Constitution.

The Constitutional Convention's job was finally done. But the Constitution was still not the law of the land. First, Congress had to review the document. After it was read out loud, the Congressmen debated it for several days.

Congress then agreed to send the Constitution along to the states. The Constitutional Convention had decided that most of the state legislatures needed to approve it. Nine out of the thirteen states had to **ratify** the U.S. Constitution before it could go into effect.

September 17, 1787
Thirty-nine members of the Constitutional Convention sign the U.S. Constitution.

September 20, 1787
The proposed Constitution is read before Congress.

Debating the document

Soon, all the state legislatures were discussing the Constitution. In every state, some legislators strongly supported the document and the changes it would make to the U.S. government. But there were also many who did not want to approve the Constitution. Most of these leaders thought giving more power to the central government would be a big mistake.

WE the People of the States of New-Hampshire, Massachusetts, Rhode-Island and Providence Plantations, Connecticut, New-York, New-Jersey, Pennsylvania, Delaware, Maryland, Virginia, North-Carolina, South-Carolina, and Georgia, do ordain, declare and establish the following Constitution for the Government of Ourselves and our Posterity.

ARTICLE I.

The stile of this Government shall be, "The United States of America."

II.

The Government shall consist of supreme legislative, executive and judicial powers.

III.

The legislative power shall be vested in a Congress, to consist of two separate and distinct bodies of men, a House of Representatives, and a Senate; ~~each of which shall, in all cases, have a negative on the other. The Legislature shall meet on the first Monday in December in every year.~~

IV.

Sect. 1. The Members of the House of Representatives shall be chosen every second year, by the people of the several States comprehended within this Union. The qualifications of the electors shall be the same, from time to time, as those of the electors in the several States, of the most numerous branch of their own legislatures.

Sect. 2. Every Member of the House of Representatives shall be of the age of twenty-five years at least; shall have been a citizen in the United States for at least ___ years before his election; and shall be, at the time of his election, ___ of the State in which he shall be chosen.

Sect. 3. The House of Representatives shall, at its first formation, and until the number of citizens and inhabitants shall be taken in the manner herein after described, consist of sixty-five Members, of whom three shall be chosen in New-Hampshire, eight in Massachusetts, one in Rhode Island and Providence Plantations, five in Connecticut, six in New-York, four in New-Jersey, eight in Pennsylvania, one in Delaware, six in Maryland, ten in Virginia, five in North-Carolina, five in South-Carolina, and three in Georgia.

Sect. 4. As the proportions of numbers in the different States will alter from time to time; as some of the States may hereafter be divided; as others may be enlarged by addition of territory; as two or more States may be united; as new States will be erected within the limits of the United States, the Legislature shall, in each of these cases, regulate the number of representatives by the number of inhabitants, according to the ___ the rate of one for every forty thousand.

Sect. 5. All bills for raising or appropriating money, and for fixing the salaries of the officers of government, shall originate in the House of Representatives, and shall not be altered or amended by the Senate. No money shall be drawn from the public Treasury, but in pursuance of appropriations that shall ___ House of Representatives.

This printed draft of the U.S. Constitution has notes written by George Washington in the margins.

Ratification

It seemed as though New York might not ratify the document. So three important supporters of the Constitution decided to take action. They were Alexander Hamilton, James Madison, and John Jay. They wrote a series of essays that were published in newspapers in New York. These famous essays are now known as the Federalist Papers. They explained why the United States needed a central government like the one described in the Constitution.

By late June 1788, nine states had ratified the U.S. Constitution. They were Delaware, Pennsylvania, New Jersey, Georgia, Connecticut, Massachusetts, Maryland, South Carolina, and New Hampshire.

Alexander Hamilton
(1755–1804)

After fighting in the **Revolutionary War**, Alexander Hamilton became a lawmaker in New York. Hamilton represented the state at the Constitutional Convention. He also contributed to the Federalist Papers, which made the case for the Constitution's **ratification**. He later served as the first secretary of the treasury and as the governor of New York.

October 27, 1787
The first of the Federalist Papers appears in print.

June 21, 1788
New Hampshire becomes the ninth state to approve the U.S. Constitution.

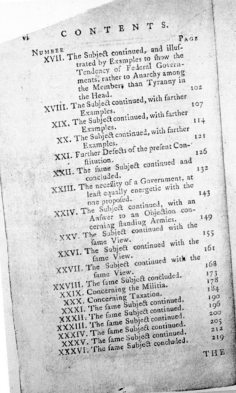

THE

FEDERALIST:

ADDRESSED TO THE

PEOPLE OF THE STATE OF
NEW-YORK.

NUMBER I.

Introduction.

AFTER an unequivocal experience of the ineffi-
cacy of the subsisting federal government, you
are called upon to deliberate on a new constitution for
the United States of America. The subject speaks its
own importance; comprehending in its consequences,
nothing less than the existence of the UNION, the
safety and welfare of the parts of which it is com-
posed, the fate of an empire, in many respects, the
most interesting in the world. It has been frequently
remarked, that it seems to have been reserved to the
people of this country, by their conduct and example,
to decide the important question, whether societies of
men are really capable or not, of establishing good
government from reflection and choice, or whether
they are forever destined to depend, for their political
constitutions, on accident and force. If there be any
truth in the remark, the crisis, at which we are arrived,
may with propriety be regarded as the æra in which
A that

The authors of the Federalist Papers supported a strong central government.

Establishing the government

However, it would still take some time before the new government would be in place. For instance, the states needed time to hold elections, so that voters could choose their representatives to Congress. Finally, on March 4, 1789, the government established by the U.S. Constitution officially began running the country. The next month, George Washington became the first president of the United States.

March 4, 1789
The national government established by the U.S. Constitution officially begins operating.

April 30, 1789
George Washington becomes the first president of the United States.

Inside the Constitution

The U.S. Constitution begins with a **preamble**, or introduction. It explains the reasons the Constitution was written. The first reason cited is "to form a more perfect Union"—in other words, to create a better country.

After the preamble are seven **articles**. The longer ones are divided into sections. The first three articles are the longest. They set out in detail how the U.S. government is structured.

Since the early 1800s, the two houses of Congress have met in the U.S. Capitol.

The first three Articles

Article I deals with **Congress**, the **legislative branch**. It explains that Congress has two houses—the House of Representatives and the Senate. It also outlines how members of Congress are selected and how long their terms in office are. The article goes into detail about exactly what powers the Congress has. These include the power to collect taxes, pay debts (money owed), regulate trade, and declare war.

Article II discusses the **executive branch**. It says who is eligible for the presidency and vice presidency and explains how these officials are elected. It also sets out the duties of the president and the reasons the president can be removed from office.

Article III focuses on the **judicial branch**. It establishes the Supreme Court as the highest court in the land.

"The executive Power shall be vested in [put in the hands of] a President of the United States of America. He shall hold his Office during the Term of four Years, and, together with the Vice President, chosen for the same Term…"

—*from Article II, Section 1, of the Constitution*

Article IV

Article IV of the U.S. Constitution deals with a variety of issues affecting states and their relationship to the U.S. government. For instance, it declares that the citizens of all states have the same rights. It also ensures that if a person commits a crime in one state and escapes to another, the person can be forced to return to the first state to stand trial. Article IV also explains how new states can be made from land claimed by the United States.

"The Senators and Representatives before mentioned…shall be bound by Oath or Affirmation, to support this Constitution…"

—*from Article VI of the Constitution*

Article V

Article V establishes ways the U.S. Constitution can be amended, or changed. One weakness of the Articles of **Confederation** was that all states had to agree to any changes to it. The Constitution instead requires that only three-fourths of the states **ratify amendments**. Because of this rule, today any amendment must be approved by 38 of the 50 states.

Articles VI and VII

Article VI confirms that the U.S. Constitution is the law of the land. It says that state **legislatures** are not allowed to make state laws in conflict with the Constitution. It also requires officials to take oaths (formal promises) to support the Constitution as they carry out their duties.

Article VII deals with the **ratification** of the Constitution. It establishes that the document has to be ratified by nine states, which it was in 1788.

*In the **engrossed** copy of the U.S. Constitution, articles were numbered using Roman numerals.*

The Bill of Rights

During the ratification process, several states insisted that the Constitution include a **bill of rights.** A bill of rights is a list of specific rights granted to the citizens of a country.

When the new Congress met, James Madison of Virginia pushed to add a bill of rights to the Constitution. He **drafted** 17 amendments. Congress then whittled them down to 10. On December 15, 1791, the 10 amendments were ratified by three-fourths of the states.

The Bill of Rights, shown here, was based on the Virginia Declaration of Rights, which the state of Virginia adopted in 1776.

The Bill of Rights ensures that Americans have many of the freedoms that some people now often take for granted. For example, the first 10 amendments grant, among other things, the right to free speech, to freedom of religion, to a fair trial, and to bear arms (weapons, particularly guns). When the Bill of Rights was added to the Constitution, they applied just to white men. Today, these rights are protected for all Americans.

"Congress shall make no law respecting an establishment of religion, or prohibiting the free exercise thereof; or abridging [reducing] the freedom of speech, or of the press; or the right of the people peaceably to assemble, and to petition the Government for a redress of grievances [complaints]."

—*The First Amendment, which is part of the Bill of Rights*

The First Amendment guarantees freedom of speech. Americans therefore cannot be put in jail for protesting against government policies.

December 15, 1791
The Bill of Rights is formally added to the Constitution.

Later amendments

The amendments in the Bill of Rights were not the last ones added to the Constitution. Today, the document includes a total of 27 amendments. Some newer amendments, however, merely canceled out older amendments. For instance, the 18th Amendment of 1920 prohibited the making and sale of alcohol in the United States. The 21st Amendment, ratified in 1933, reversed the 18th, making alcohol legal again.

"The right of citizens of the United States to vote shall not be denied or abridged [restricted] by the United States or by any State on account of sex [being male or female]."

—from the 19th Amendment to the Constitution

Other changes

There are other important amendments, too. The 13th Amendment abolished (ended) slavery. The 16th Amendment authorized a federal (national) income tax. The 22nd Amendment limited presidents to only two four-year terms in office.

The 15th Amendment allowed African American men to participate in elections starting in 1870.

Voting rights

Several of the most significant amendments have to do with voting rights. For instance, the 15th Amendment said that **race** could not disqualify anyone from voting. The right to vote was extended to U.S. women through the 19th Amendment. The 26th Amendment lowered the voting age to 18.

Women fought to be able to vote in U.S. elections for decades before the 19th Amendment gave them this right in 1920.

Preserving the Past

After the Constitution was **ratified**, the **engrossed** copy was given to Thomas Jefferson for safekeeping. At that time, he was the secretary of state, an important official who oversees the dealings of the United States with foreign countries. In 1800 when Washington, D.C., became the national capital, the Constitution was placed in storage there.

Saving the Constitution

At one time, the document might have been lost forever if not for the quick thinking of James Monroe. When he was secretary of state, the United States was at war with Great Britain. The conflict was called the War of 1812, although it lasted from 1812 to 1814.

In 1814 British troops descended on Washington, D.C., and set fire to many buildings there, including the White House. As Monroe fled the city, he saved the U.S. Constitution and the Declaration of Independence. He stuffed them in a sack and carried them from the capital with him.

1800
The Constitution is stored in Washington, D.C.

1814
James Monroe saved the Constitution by taking it out of Washington, D.C., during the War of 1812. It is later returned to Washington.

Visitors to the National Archives can see the official copies of the U.S. Constitution, the Bill of Rights, and the Declaration of Independence in the Charters of Freedom exhibit.

On display

After the War of 1812, the documents were returned to Washington. But the U.S. Constitution was not put on public display until 1924. The staff of the Library of **Congress** placed it on view in a special protective case.

In 1952 the Constitution was transferred to the National **Archives** in Washington, D.C. Visitors to the archives' Charters of Freedom exhibit can now view all four pages of the engrossed Constitution. Nearby cases hold the Declaration of Independence and the **Bill of Rights**.

1924
The Constitution is put on display in the Library of Congress in Washington, D.C.

1952
The Constitution is displayed in the National Archives in Washington, D.C.

Conservators

Before the Constitution was placed in its display case at the National Archives, employees carefully examined it. They were **conservators**—experts at restoring and protecting old documents. The Constitution was in fairly good shape, but it did show some signs of age. The surface of the **parchment** was uneven, so they stretched it out. Some ink was also flaking off. They carefully reattached the flakes with a tiny brush.

Conservators must have a clear eye and steady hand when restoring fragile documents.

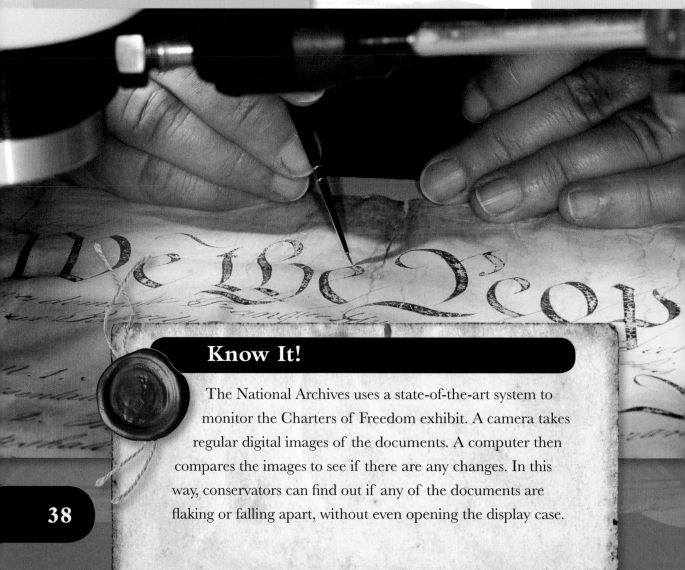

Know It!

The National Archives uses a state-of-the-art system to monitor the Charters of Freedom exhibit. A camera takes regular digital images of the documents. A computer then compares the images to see if there are any changes. In this way, conservators can find out if any of the documents are flaking or falling apart, without even opening the display case.

Archiving the past

Archivists also treat important documents such as the U.S. Constitution with special care. In museums and historical societies across the country, their job involves making sure all types of **primary sources** are available for future generations to see.

In addition to storing these items properly, they also study the letters, diaries, and other documents in their collections. They try to discover everything they can about the history of these primary sources. The more archivists understand these items, the more they can help visitors to their archives research different topics. Archivists also share their knowledge through exhibits of the items in their collections.

The U.S. Constitution Today

In the hands of the skilled staff at the National **Archives**, the **engrossed** copy of the Constitution is well preserved. Although it shows some damage, it looks almost like it did when it was first created.

Constitutional amendments

The Constitution is more than just a **parchment** document. It is also a plan for the operation of the U.S. government, and that has changed a good deal over time.

Through the addition of 27 **amendments**, the Constitution has grown longer and more complicated. It deals with issues no one even thought about at the Constitutional **Convention**. In this way, as the country and the needs of its people have grown, the amendment process has allowed the Constitution to adapt to changing times.

"The judicial Power of the United States shall be vested in [put in the hands of] one supreme Court, and in such inferior Courts as the **Congress** may from time to time ordain and establish."

—*from Article III of the Constitution*

Legal challenges

The Supreme Court was first established through **Article** III of the document. Since that time, that court has heard many cases. Some involve questions about whether laws follow the rules outlined in the Constitution. If the Supreme Court finds a law unconstitutional, it can be struck down.

Through these cases, judges and legal experts have examined and reexamined the Constitution. Sometimes, in the face of new legal questions, they come to interpret the words in the Constitution in a new and different way.

Every year, cases decided by the Supreme Court change the ways experts understand the Constitution.

Other constitutions

Because the Constitution has changed with changing times, it has survived for more than 220 years. It is now one of the oldest constitutions of any government in the world.

Throughout the years, it has inspired many other countries to write their own constitutions. Today, there are about 100 democratic nations, which have governments run for and by the people. Many have a written constitution. Some of those are modeled directly on the U.S. Constitution.

Barack Obama is the 44th president to pledge to uphold the U.S. Constitution.

"We the People"

When the **Founding Fathers** wrote the Constitution, they had no idea how long it would last. After all, the Articles of **Confederation** had been in use for just 11 years. The men who wrote the Constitution would likely be amazed that the form of government they created has lasted more than 20 times longer.

The Founding Fathers might even be surprised that the United States has survived all these years. After all, when the country was first established, it was built on a new and untried idea. Following the **Revolutionary War**, Americans did not want to be ruled by a king or by a small group of wealthy people. They wanted to choose their own leaders and wanted those leaders to serve all Americans.

No other country had ever had that type of government before. In this way, the United States was an experiment. And the U.S. Constitution is one of the most important reasons that experiment has been a success.

Timeline

May 14, 1607
Jamestown, the first permanent British settlement in what is now the United States, is founded.

December 16, 1773
American colonists protest British taxes at the Boston Tea Party.

April 19, 1775
The Revolutionary War begins with the battles of Lexington and Concord.

May 25, 1787
The Philadelphia Convention (now known as the Constitutional Convention) begins.

May 14, 1787
Delegates from all the states, except for Rhode Island, gather in Philadelphia to discuss revising the Articles of Confederation.

September 11, 1786
State representatives meet for the Annapolis Convention.

May 29, 1787
Delegates from Virginia present the Virginia Plan to the Convention.

June 13, 1787
Convention delegates create the first draft of the Constitution.

June 23, 1787
Convention delegates establish the Committee of Detail to revise the Constitution.

March 4, 1789
The national government established by the U.S. Constitution officially begins operating.

June 21, 1788
New Hampshire becomes the ninth state to approve the U.S. Constitution.

October 27, 1787
The first of the Federalist Papers appears in print.

April 30, 1789
George Washington becomes the first president of the United States.

December 15, 1791
The Bill of Rights is formally added to the Constitution.

1800
The Constitution is stored in Washington, D.C.

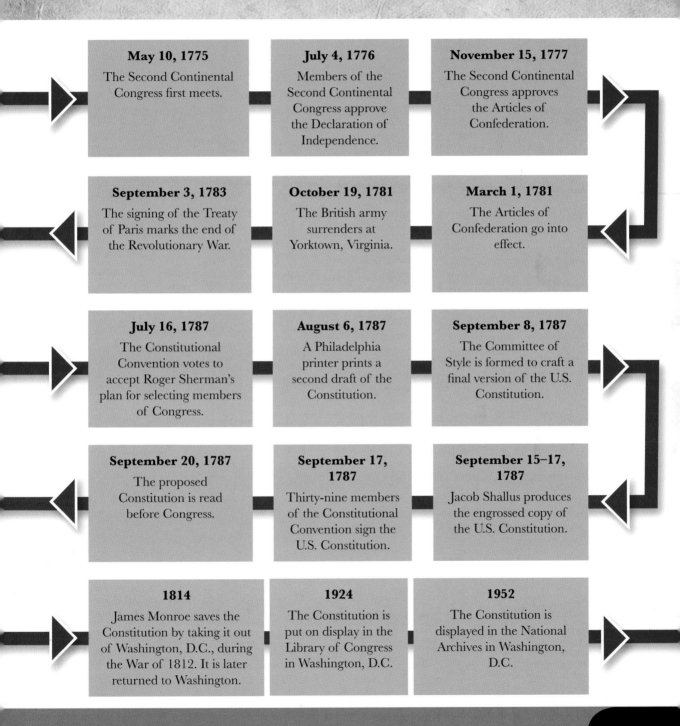

May 10, 1775
The Second Continental Congress first meets.

July 4, 1776
Members of the Second Continental Congress approve the Declaration of Independence.

November 15, 1777
The Second Continental Congress approves the Articles of Confederation.

September 3, 1783
The signing of the Treaty of Paris marks the end of the Revolutionary War.

October 19, 1781
The British army surrenders at Yorktown, Virginia.

March 1, 1781
The Articles of Confederation go into effect.

July 16, 1787
The Constitutional Convention votes to accept Roger Sherman's plan for selecting members of Congress.

August 6, 1787
A Philadelphia printer prints a second draft of the Constitution.

September 8, 1787
The Committee of Style is formed to craft a final version of the U.S. Constitution.

September 20, 1787
The proposed Constitution is read before Congress.

September 17, 1787
Thirty-nine members of the Constitutional Convention sign the U.S. Constitution.

September 15–17, 1787
Jacob Shallus produces the engrossed copy of the U.S. Constitution.

1814
James Monroe saves the Constitution by taking it out of Washington, D.C., during the War of 1812. It is later returned to Washington.

1924
The Constitution is put on display in the Library of Congress in Washington, D.C.

1952
The Constitution is displayed in the National Archives in Washington, D.C.

Glossary

amendment change or addition to an official document

archive place that holds a collection of historical documents and other primary sources

archivist expert who works in an archive

article portion of an official or legal document

bill of rights list of specific rights granted to the citizens of a country

colonist person who lives in a colony

colony area controlled by another country

confederation group of countries, states, or territories bound together in an alliance

Congress lawmaking body of the U.S. government

conservator expert who repairs and restores old documents

convention large meeting

delegate person sent to a meeting to represent others

draft early version of a document; also, to write an early version of a document

engross to create the final version of a legal document

executive branch part of the U.S. government that oversees its day-to-day operations

Founding Fathers men who ruled the United States in its earliest years, especially those who signed the U.S. Constitution

judicial branch part of the U.S. government that deals with court cases of national importance

legislative branch part of the U.S. government that makes national laws

legislature government body that makes laws

parchment thin, paper-like material

preamble introduction

primary source document or object made in the past that provides information about a certain time

race group of people defined by their physical characteristics

ratification official approval of a formal document

ratify approve

revise change

Revolutionary War war fought by American colonists from 1775 to 1783 to win independence from British rule

secondary source account written by someone who studied primary sources

Find Out More

Books

Fradin, Dennis Brindell. *The Signers: The 56 Stories Behind the Declaration of Independence*. New York: Walker, 2003.

Freedman, Russell. *In Defense of Liberty: The Story of America's Bill of Rights*. New York: Holiday House, 2003.

Ransom, Candice F. *Who Wrote the U.S. Constitution? And Other Questions About the Constitutional Convention of 1787*. Minneapolis, Minn.: Lerner, 2010.

Stein, R. Conrad. *The National Archives*. New York: Franklin Watts, 2002.

Taylor-Butler, Christine. *The Constitution of the United States*. New York: Children's Press, 2008.

Websites

The Charters of Freedom: The National Archives
www.archives.gov/exhibits/charters
This website features images of various versions of the Constitution and biographies of the Founding Fathers.

Creating the United States: The Library of Congress
http://myloc.gov/Exhibitions/creatingtheus/Pages/default.aspx
Visit this website to learn how the U.S. Constitution was created.

To Form a More Perfect Union: The Library of Congress
http://memory.loc.gov/ammem/collections/continental/intro01.html
This site discusses the Constitutional Convention and the events leading up to it.

Index